READ THIS

TILL YOU

BELIEVE IT

WRITTEN BY: M.H. CLARK

DESIGNED BY: JESSICA PHOENIX

RIGHT NOW IS A HARD TIME.

YOU DON'T HAVE TO LOVE IT. YOU DON'T HAVE TO DO THIS GRACEFULLY. YOU DON'T HAVE TO FIND WHAT'S GOOD IN THIS MOMENT. YOU JUST HAVE TO MAKE IT THROUGH.

THESE WORDS ARE HERE TO HELP YOU GET THERE.

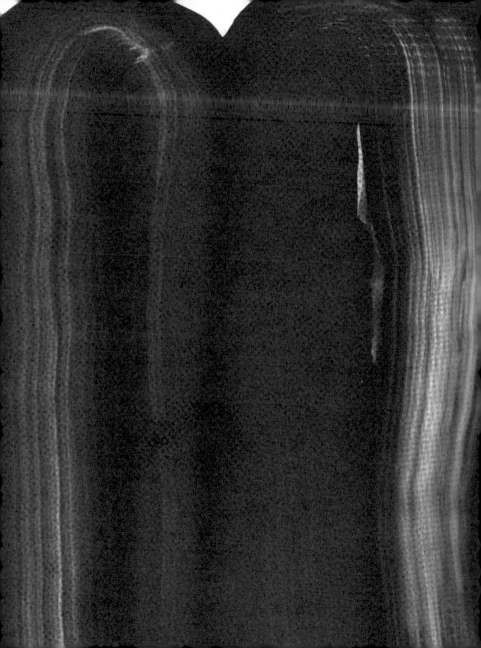

NO MATTER WHAT HAS
HAPPENED, NO MATTER
HOW YOU FEEL RIGHT NOW,
YOU ARE STILL YOU.

EVEN

THROUGH

THIS.

YOU ARE STILL
INFINITELY
COMPLEX.

YOU ARE STILL BIGGER

THAN THIS FEELING.

THERE IS
MORE TO YOU
THAN THIS
MOMENT.

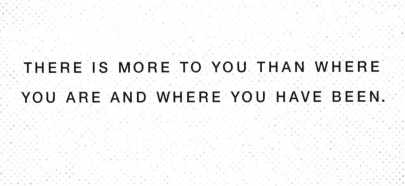

THERE IS MORE TO YOU THAN WHERE YOU ARE AND WHERE YOU HAVE BEEN.

THIS IS ANOTHER
PART OF YOUR
STORY. THIS IS NOT
THE WHOLE STORY.

EVERYTHING
YOU ARE,
EVERYTHING YOU HAVE
ALREADY LIVED THROUGH,
MAKES YOU ABLE TO
WEATHER THIS STORM.

THERE IS NO SHAME IN GRIEF, AND NO DISGRACE

IN SORROW, AND NO WEAKNESS IN DESPAIR.

THIS
FEELING
MEANS
YOUR
HEART
WORKS.

THIS FEELING
MEANS YOU HAVE
LIVED FULLY AND
LOVED DEEPLY.

HONOR WHAT'S BEEN LOST.

GIVE YOURSELF TIME.

TAKE AS
LONG
AS YOU
NEED.

SOMETIMES, YOU CAN TAKE LIFE A DAY AT A TIME. SOMETIMES, YOU CAN TAKE JUST AN HOUR AT A TIME. AND SOMETIMES, ALL YOU CAN DO IS THIS VERY MOMENT, HAND OVER HAND, UNTIL THE NEXT MOMENT IS GIVEN.

IN THESE TIMES,

BE VERY
GENTLE TO
YOURSELF.

IT WILL NOT BE THIS DIFFICULT FOREVER.

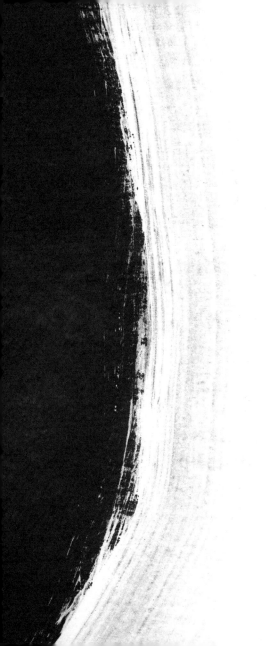

YOU WILL
NOT BE
FOREVER
IN THE
DARK.

IT MAY SEEM SMALL,
IT MAY SEEM DISTANT,
BUT THERE IS LIGHT
FOR YOU HERE.

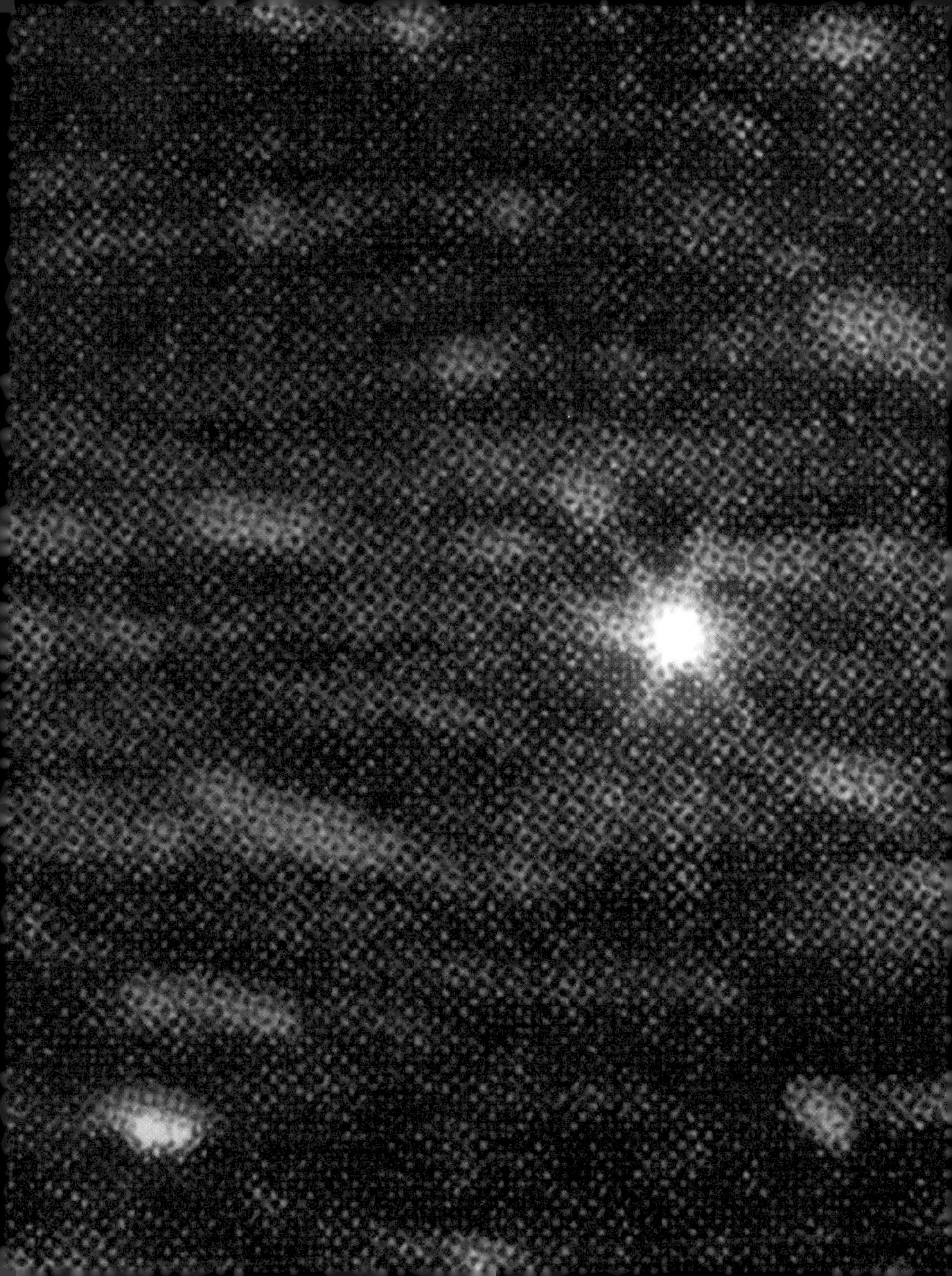

YOUR HEALING MAY NOT
OCCUR IN A STRAIGHT LINE.

YOU ARE STILL HERE. YOU ARE ON YOUR WAY.

JUST BY LIVING, JUST BY CONTINUING,

YOUR HEALING HAS BEGUN.

A BRIGHT MOMENT
DOES NOT DISHONOR
YOUR LOSS.

A DIFFICULT MOMENT
DOES NOT DISHONOR
YOUR JOY.

THERE IS STILL LIFE IN THE

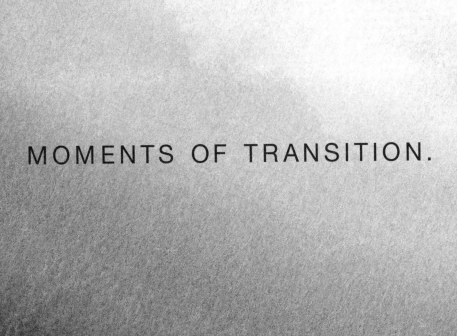

MOMENTS OF TRANSITION.

YOU CAN DO A LOT, BUT YOU
CANNOT DO EVERYTHING.

FORGIVE YOURSELF.

COME HOME
TO
YOURSELF.

YOU HAVE AN INCREDIBLE AMOUNT
OF LIFE POURED INTO YOU.

IT FILLS YOU
TO THE TOP.

YOUR LIFE IS STILL
A STORY OF JOY AND
COMPLEXITY, TRIAL
AND OVERCOMING.

YOU CAN STILL CREATE
WHAT COMES NEXT.

AND WHAT'S NEXT IS
WORTHWHILE.

IT MAY BE MESSY. IT MAY BE PAINFUL. IT MAY BE COMPLICATED.

AND IT IS STILL

WORTHWHILE.

YOU CAN LIVE THIS MOMENT

INTO THE NEXT.

COMPENDIUM.
live inspired

WRITTEN BY: M.H. CLARK
DESIGNED BY: JESSICA PHOENIX
EDITED BY: AMELIA RIEDLER AND KRISTIN EADE

ISBN: 978-1-938298-98-1

11TH PRINTING. PRINTED IN CHINA WITH SOY INKS ON FSC®-MIX CERTIFIED PAPER.

*Create
meaningful
moments
with gifts
that inspire.*

CONNECT WITH US
live-inspired.com | sayhello@compendiuminc.com

@compendiumliveinspired
#compendiumliveinspired